THE GIFT OF CHOICE

Presenting a different possibility for creating
ease with death and dying

By Wendy Mulder

Dying Happy
Copyright © 2014 Wendy Mulder
ISBN: 978-1-939261-95-3

All rights reserved. No part of this publication may be reproduced, stored in a retrieval system, or transmitted, in any form or by any means, electronic, mechanical, photocopying, recording or otherwise without prior written permission from the publisher.

The author and publisher of the book do not make any claim or guarantee for any physical, mental, emotional, spiritual, or financial result. All products, services and information provided by the author are for general education and entertainment purposes only. The information provided herein is in no way a substitute for medical or other professional advice. In the event you use any of the information contained in this book for yourself, the author and publisher assume no responsibility for your actions.

Published by
Access Consciousness Publishing, LLC
www.accessconsciousnesspublishing.com

Printed in the United States of America

Prologue

If you have questions about how to care for someone who is dying…

This is for you.

If you are wondering if there is a different possibility to what is presented by mainstream organisations…

This is for you.

If somewhere inside you know it is possible to have ease with death, and yet, at the same time it feels impossible right now…

This is for you.

If you would like to have no regrets about your choices as a caregiver…

This is for you.

Contents

Introduction vii

Diary 13

Epilogue 45

Summary of Access Tools 51

Mum's Gifts 53

Would You Like to Know More? 55

Testimonials 57

About the Author 59

Other Books 61

Introduction

This is a very personal diary about my mum dying at home and me being her caregiver during that time. It's a raw and real account of what happened, and it's one person's intimate experience of a very different way of being with someone as they die.

Whether you are the caregiver, or you are close to someone who is dying, this journal offers insights into what else is possible if you take the path less travelled. Your journey will be different.

And while you may not think so right now, the process of dying can have an incredible amount of ease for everyone involved. This journal invites you to explore that possibility in a very real way, knowing that every choice creates different possibilities. And while you can't get it wrong, your choices can create more ease than you could ever imagine!

I am making this available publicly because a lot of people have said to me, "Oh, I wish I had done that for my mum. I wish I had done that for my dad." But they didn't have trust in themselves that something different actually could be possible.

If you would like to know you have choices in this process, rather than go into the "should-do, have-to, and got-to" approaches tradition suggests, this is one way forward.

You have choices for how you care for a dying person. This is a journey that can be honouring of everyone, and that can work for everyone involved. Instead of losing yourself in caring for your loved one, you can receive gifts in the process. What if you could receive the gift of having no regrets? The gift of being you, no matter what is going on around you?

Every choice is good for just ten seconds; understand you can change your mind at any time. Please don't hold onto your points of view. As your situation changes, so will the essence of what is going to work; being flexible is part of what creates the ease.

Personally, the gift of choice was trusting that I could be all of me, while still being a contribution to my mum. It was very clear that I didn't have to compromise my life and living in any way. Having this awareness and clarity, allowed me to not be embroiled in any trauma and drama of what Mum was choosing. These choices created the ease!

If you are caring for everyone except you, it is draining and exhausting. If you are participating in trauma and drama instead of caring and ease, your energy is misdirected and you miss out on the beauty and vulnerability you could have with your loved one as they pass.

First choosing caring and nurturing for you allows you to become the ripple effect for everyone involved. What contribution can you be that you have never imagined?

One of the things I know for sure is that in life, you need a selection of tools in your toolbag to assist with finding ease in many of the situations you are faced with; tradesmen cannot effectively build anything without the right tools. Dealing with grief and loss is no different. When you have the right tools, the journey can be one of more ease and peace, for you and for the person you are caring for. The tools I used during the process of caring for my mum were invaluable. All too often in times of stress we lack the presence of Being, which leads to disconnection from ourselves and from others. The tools of Access Consciousness® helped me to remain present and conscious throughout the process, allowing me to gain more awareness around dying, disease, relationships and the significance we place on life and death and everything in between.

Access Consciousness® is a set of tools and philosophies that can assist you in freeing yourself from the constraints of things like judgment, guilt and conclusion. These tools allow for greater possibilities to show up for every life situation. The founder of Access Consciousness®, Gary Douglas, says that consciousness includes everything and judges nothing. The mantra for Access Consciousness® is, *"All of life comes to me with ease, joy and glory."* Throughout this journal, I will share some of the tools I used to help create more ease for my mum during her process of dying.

As I look back on my journey, I am grateful for the rare peace that comes with having no regrets. As you enter this space for yourself, I invite you to share in my experience. I hope the tools I share with you throughout this diary allow for far more ease than you thought was possible.

The important thing is not to stop questioning.
Curiosity has its own reason for existing.

~ Albert Einstein

March 2009: Where do we begin?

Mum has been using "Fentanyl patches" now for a week. Her pain appears to be less. She says it's from her tummy up that she feels sick all the time. She is not eating, and feels light-headed and dizzy.

Dad isn't well either. He looks pale and tired and is feeling unwell. If I didn't know better, I'd feel he is trying to beat her to the Pearly Gates so he isn't the one left behind. He avoids talking about her cancer, though his whole body language is:

"How can I live without her?"

"I don't know anything else."

"She is my life."

It is interesting to observe and serves as a great reminder to me to be aware of not completely losing yourself in your partner and having no life for yourself, no matter how long you have been together.

It is a reminder to contribute to myself. One of the things I put in place early on in the role of caring for Mum was setting up a phone tree. It's exhausting talking on the phone to all the family members with regular updates from doctors' visits; too much repetition of the story.

Instead, I assigned my sister the role of passing on all the information to everybody. This is something she is happy to do, and which she does well. This frees me up and allows me more space and ease. I did this with my friends too, which worked out well; I have a friend who keeps everyone up-to-date, and I phone when I can.

Tool #1 ~ Asking Questions

Being a caregiver can often be misidentified as a doing. There are many things that need doing as part of caring for a dying person. But the result of being caught up in doing instead of being is often exhaustion. Asking questions without any conclusion of what the answer should be, allows what is required to show up for you.

I recommend you start each day with some simple self-inquiry questions like:

- *What is required of me today?*
- *How can I do it with ease?*
- *What choice could I make that I never thought possible?*
- *Is this a choice I would like to make?*
- *Is there another choice that would work even better?*

Some days you may get the awareness that nothing is required and you can then choose some time out for yourself.

Trust in your own awareness to ask questions continually.

March 13th: Doing the runaround.

Mum went for a bone scan this morning. After the bone scan I dropped her off at home, fixed some lunch, then took Dad for his afternoon appointments. She was sleeping when we left.

When 5:00 pm arrives, Dad is still with me, and I realize it would be silly to drive him home and then go back and pick up the reports. I leave him in the car while I duck in and pick them up.

I quickly scan the reports—it shows she has metastasis in her bones. I'm in denial, thinking, "I'll read it properly when I get home." The words of the report aren't gelling.

Back in the car, Dad asks, "Can you read the report?"

I say, "No Dad, I can't read it properly. We'll have to wait until Monday to see the doctor, and he'll tell us then."

That satisfies him for now. My next challenge will be convincing Mum I don't know what the report says! The day is starting to take its toll. I've been going since early morning, doing stuff with both Mum and Dad.

We need to go to the chemist for Mum on our way home. I arrive at the chemist, and the girl behind the counter asks about my mum. That is the end of me; tears come flowing.

I walk around the shop for another ten minutes so I have stopped crying enough to get back in the car with Dad. I don't stay long with Mum. I keep it short and tell her the same as I told Dad. She seems happy with that for now.

I arrive home and then have a good cry. I need this time for me to grieve. I am in no state to talk to anyone except my immediate family. I ask for no one to call and thankfully no one does. It's my time to digest the information, and I'm grateful for this.

A few days later, I tell my parents the results I read on the report. I don't want it to be a surprise when they see the doctor on Monday. My brother is with me for support.

April 10th: What else is there?

Today we have a doctor's appointment to learn what else is possible with Mum's condition. In the appointment, Mum asks the doctor, "How long do I have to live?"

"You won't make the year," he replies.

Mum looks at me in shock. Even though she knows she is dying, it is still a shock to actually hear the words.

She's grateful Dad isn't in the room yet. Dad arrives to hear that we will be trying something different to help her with the nausea. He is happy about this: to him it means Mum may be able to eat more, which means she may get better. Dad can't see the truth about Mum dying.

He is completely oblivious to how Mum is feeling. I must hand it to her — she's had ninety-four years of practising being the chameleon, so he doesn't really see how miserable and in shock she's feeling.

For me, I see how much energy it takes out of her to hide it all from Dad. It's so much easier to be yourself no matter what it looks like.

Thank you, Mum, for showing and reminding me of that so clearly.

Tool #2 ~ Allowance

Most people like to be in control of situations around them so they know what's coming next and what to expect. One of the things I realized when caring for my mum was that you never control anything. And so, I used the Access Consciousness® "Allowance" tool. This tool means everything is just an interesting point of view. Situations, treatment options, prognosis and requirements can change from minute to minute. Sometimes the need to change direction can be so overwhelming that it's difficult to keep up. Feelings of guilt and despair can creep in when things aren't going as you expected, and the only way to effectively deal with this is by being in a constant state of allowance.

Don't get stuck on a point of view that was only valid for that moment. Be in allowance for change and continually ask questions like, "What else is possible?" and "What's right about this that I'm not getting?"

When you are in allowance, you are present. When you are present, you are better able to listen to what is being said to you. Allowance also allows you to be better equipped to get others to listen to you.

The most valuable awareness I had throughout the whole process was being in allowance of ME. I was doing the best I could with what I had at the time. There is no good or bad, right or wrong. Stay out of judgment of yourself, stay in allowance of yourself and trust your own knowing. You are already amazing.

April 25th: The dreaded "How are you?" question.

It's Sunday morning, and I'm still at home. I don't ring Mum as much anymore because I can hear in her voice how unwell she is. I feel for the rest of the family because when they get off the phone with her, they are left with the lifeless energy she often represents.

It is easier for me to just drive the few minutes to their home and see them face to face. Besides, it's pointless asking, "How are you?" to someone who's dying, or as Mum calls it, "On her last leg of the journey."

This road now is what scares her the most. Being in pain and feeling sick at the same time, losing her independence and ownership of life, getting lost in the hospital system and not coming out and having to depend on others for everything. Actual death and leaving her body doesn't concern her; death isn't the bogeyman to her.

How much better could it be if we could leave this life without having to have our body degenerate in the process?

Today, we talk about what she would like for her funeral.

"I don't care, I won't be here," she says. She isn't interested in the ritual of a funeral, and she sees no point in having a lot of hoo-hah.

Mum has always been a Baptist, which I didn't know until today.

I ask her, "Mum, I have found this nice minister. Would you like to talk to him?"

"I'm fine. I already talked to God, and he knows what I am asking," she replies.

I ask her if are there any wishes she would like, or does she want to be dressed in anything particular when she dies. She replies: "No, do whatever you like!"

Mum then remarks, "It is the ones left behind that are sad, if they choose to be sad. But not me, I'll be at peace and happy. I have lived a long life, and I have survived and thrived through many challenges. This one I won't, and I am happy to go."

To me this said it all.

I acknowledge the celebration of being alive and enjoy the present moment with my mum.

Mum reminds me of a time I was very ill as a child. She had stayed with me for days, never leaving my bedside in the hospital. Everyone kept telling her I would die. She prayed to God saying, "If Wendy isn't going to get better and will only be in pain, let her go."

This was now my prayer, for me to let go of her and to allow her to choose. We had come full circle.

Tool #3 ~ Gratitude

If I told you there was something greater than love, would you want to know what it is? Especially when you are caring for a loved one who is dying, if there is anything greater than love, now is the time to find out what it is! The answer is gratitude.

Yes, gratitude truly is greater than love. To have gratitude for someone means you have no judgment, of them or yourself. When emotions are high, we can all become challenging to deal with, and we can all feel challenged by others. But when you are grateful for someone, regardless of if they are being kind, happy, sad or angry, you can't judge them and react to them.

When you are in gratitude, you can't judge yourself either. Having gratitude allows you to move through the day with more ease. The moment you are in reaction to someone or something, you are in judgment. When you are in judgment, you are no longer in gratitude.

May 8th: The naturalness and inclusiveness of dying with family.

Mum is now living with me and my family. I am very aware of the change in her condition and how it will continue to decline. Dad is away with my brother David. They have gone to see some properties out West.

Mum has requested that Dad goes. She sees how upset and depressed he is, seeing her so unwell, and she doesn't want to cause him any more pain. She knows how much he loves the open space and fresh air of the bush. If he is happy, then so is she.

When Mum came to stay with us, I chose that, no matter what happened, I would face it with as much ease as possible.

I've done the hard, uncomfortable, stressed and tired bit well enough to know that it doesn't work for me.

Instead, I asked what gifts I could receive from this time with my mum and time with all my extended family members. What an honour for me to be able to gift to my mum her final wish of being able to stay at home!

Not long after Mum arrived, my eldest son Luke came back to live at home—with glandular fever.

Our house is becoming very full. Luckily for me my husband, Siemon, is home to help out.

As it turned out, it is truly wonderful having everyone under the same roof; the whole family gets to participate and have time with Mum. Lots of family members visit as they choose. We continue on with our lives.

My son, Paul, goes to school, and the joke is that it's Mum lying in bed who reminds us to pick up Paul from sport and his other events.

My sister comes on the weekends to relieve me and help out with the cleaning. My brothers take over the role of looking after Dad, and when he returns from his trip, one of them is there to bring him over to our house.

The community nurse still comes over once a week. She calls it a "support visit," and she has a chat with Mum to see how Mum is doing.

I marvel at Mum. I had an agenda that the community nurses care for mum daily, but Mum's agenda is very different. She has it in her head that I'll be the caring nurse all the way to the end. She is and always has been a private person and trusts me with her care, and I don't have the heart to force her to do it my way. I suppose she wasn't called a Colonel for no reason!

The early months were a constant battle to get her to allow services to come to her home to see what safety aids like support rails, alarms and bed sticks could be installed.

Different services came to gather information before making assessments. Mum would last about ten minutes before she'd leave the room.

Mum would say, "I don't feel well so I'm going to sit down. Anyway, I can't hear what they're saying."

Her body language clearly said, "I'm not interested, so what's the point?"

I would be left giving all the personal information on Mum and at the same time trying to understand how the different departments work, who is in charge of what and how the departments work together. Welcome to the confusing Queensland Health Department!

I wished I could claim deafness as well.

Tool #4 ~ Uncreate and Destroy Your Relationships

I think it's fair to say that if you are caring for a dying family member, particularly parents, there is likely to be some unresolved issues between you. It can be challenging for both of you as you navigate your way through emotions that may arise and dealing with the fact they now require your complete empathy and compassion. One of the Access Consciousness® tools I found useful is the process of "uncreating and destroying" your relationship with that person.

Say you are having a bad day with someone; they've pushed your buttons, and you've reacted. In that moment, you make a whole heap of judgments about them. Who they are, what they've "done" and how they've made you "feel." And quite possibly, they've made the same conclusions about you.

With all the judgments and conclusions you've both come to, you've effectively "stuck" each other in those judgments. You wake up the next day, and without even being cognitively aware of it, you relate to that person from those judgments.

When you destroy and uncreate your relationship every day, you are asking for all the judgments you've made to be destroyed and the reality you've created from those judgments to be uncreated. It's a way of clearing the energy to start again every single day. Removing the judgments and conclusions allows both of you to show up differently than before. You begin to see people differently, for who they truly are. This tool is also useful for dealing with family members and friends who are also involved in the care giving process.

May 10th: Mother's Day.

What a day! Bedlam is the best way to describe it. Mum's sister, Frances, died this morning at 1:30 am—she was ninety-three. The morning started with phone calls galore—some to wish Mum, "Happy Mother's Day" and some to let her know about her sister.

I was feeling vulnerable from all the hype on TV and in the shops about Mother's Day. Buy this for your mother! Go there, do this! And on and on it goes.

Is this one day the ONLY day of the year you're supposed to make your mother feel special?

I'm feeling all the stuff people are experiencing on Mother's Day. I start asking myself, "Well, what about you, what are you doing? What's your family doing for you? Everybody else is out having a good time." I see how easy it is to get caught up in it all.

My family is supporting me in the best way possible—laying low. They are aware their mum is taken up with their nanna, and they help out where they can.

After things settle down in the morning, I shower Mum for the first time in a week. Everything is going fine until it is time to get her out of the shower.

I can see the signs; head down, no response to calling her name, slumping over in the shower chair.

She's done this to me once before at her own home when dad was away, so I act quickly. Luckily, I have Siemon around this time who is strong enough to lift her out of the shower and get her back to bed as quickly as possible. Once back in her bed, she comes round again quite quickly.

"No more showers!" I tell her. She has been asking me all week for a shower but after that episode it is my time to be the boss!

Later that day, we help her to the chair in the lounge so she could visit with us. Later, she actually walks back to her room unassisted! How things change from one minute to the next.

Tool #5 ~ Get Your Bars™ Run

One of the very first processes I learned from Access Consciousness® was a treatment called The Access Consciousness Bars™. It involves gently touching different points on the head. A typical treatment can last anywhere from an hour to an hour and a half. A treatment is literally life changing.

Our points of view and perspective create the reality we experience and the way we see life. Many of these points of view are locked in from a very early age — or even other lifetimes. Having your Bars™ run helps to energetically unlock those points of view, allowing you to relax and see the world differently. Things literally begin to show up differently than they ever have before.

If you have some points of view about dying, disease or caring for someone who is dying that are getting in the way of finding peace with the situation, you may find The Bars™ to be a useful tool. The Bars™ not only give you some time away from the stress to relax, but also assist you with shifting some of those points of view to allow for different possibilities.

May 23rd: Acknowledgment.

I remember a great friend of mine saying, "To find the strength for tomorrow be conscious and present in the moment called now." Mum is awake and coughing early this morning, finding it very uncomfortable. She makes the comment, "I keep praying to God to take me, I am not going to get better so we might as well get the job done!" Sounds familiar. She also says, "I can't help Dad anymore so the sooner I go the better."

I ask her if she feels sad now.

"No," she says. She chuckles then says, "We'll all have a job ahead of us sorting everything out."

I'm not quite sure what she means by that. Could it be Dad?

May 24th: Trust.

Words, words, words. What do they mean when all your energy is taken up with that next valuable breath? Mum has a moist cough now. It's like she is drowning in her own phlegm. Part of me wants to take her to the hospital where she can have assistance to help her, though I know that's not her wish.

I am up and down through the night. My bed is the floor. (I am amazed at how comfortable it is, not being one usually for sleeping on floors!) I am grateful to have the strength to stay with it.

Mum knowingly voices her gratitude. It becomes an awareness to know what to do and when; not to get caught up in the trauma and drama of what is happening. I hear the birds. They sing a soft tune. I feel the soft breeze coming through the window, bringing with it the scent of the flowers. The sun breaks through; it's doing what it always does—shining bright.

The joys of a new day and being alive, while at the same time seeing another life ebbing away. I leave Mum for a bit while everyone sleeps. I ring my good friend, and we have our early morning chat, both of us being early birds. It's great having support, and I cherish these calls.

She lets me know she's keeping everyone up-to-date with Mum's condition and how they all send their love. The rest of the family is coming today. I told them I don't think it will be long, although no one really knows.

May 26th: Thank you for that breath.

Another night sleeping on the floor. My sister, Pam, is here with me; she is sleeping in the lounge. Dad is over at the apartment with other family members. Siemon helped me reposition Mum several times during the night. I wake Pam as I bang the kettle on the kitchen bench, declaring loudly, "Mum, how much longer are you going to go on with this?"

The look of horror on my sister's face of, "How could I say such a thing?" breaks me into fits of laughter. It's priceless! I think it shocks her enough to go and sit with Mum while I enjoy my cuppa by myself!

Pam has never found it easy being around sickness or dying—it's something she would prefer to stay away from. I feel a lot changes for her during this time with Mum. And, as with many of the family members, Pam gets to see that death isn't something to be scared of or avoid. The only two things we are certain of in this life are birth and death—what we make of that in between is up to us.

At 6:00 am I wake my younger son, Paul, to get ready for school. His older brother, Luke, is still asleep. Both the boys are aware Nanna could go anytime. They have their special goodnight chats with Mum before bed. Luke's cheeky humour every morning is, "Good morning, Nanna. You're still alive!" She gives him one of her beautiful smiles, which he loves and they both have a big laugh.

I ask Mum if she minds if I ring the doctor to come and check on her. He is due to come during his lunch hour, but I'd like him to check on her this morning.

Straight away, Mum is not happy about it. Still being Little Miss Independent! I reassure her it is only to see if he can make her a little more comfortable, and I won't allow her to be sent off to the hospital. She agrees to it with good grace.

Mum had been a nurse for many years. She knows how easily the hospital system takes over, and you lose your control and freedom as an individual. Up to now Mum has had very little pain. "The patches" and Panadol keep her pain controlled. It's more the cough and her piles that make her feel uncomfortable.

Her doctor arrives at 7:30 am. I'm grateful to him for the care, consideration and willingness to go that extra step to give her comfort, ease and respect. Over the last month, it is a great comfort to me to know he is only a phone call away if I need him.

She tells the doctor, "I'm still here" and proceeds to tell him the story about how she got the piles. She can hardly talk, but to her, it's a story he needs to hear. He patiently listens and then suggests giving her a little injection to take away the discomfort. He says he'll be back at lunchtime to check on her.

Mum finally "got her job done!" She died peacefully at 8:30 am. That breath that gives life was suddenly no longer there. She quietly left her body. For me, there are tears of sadness, as well as great joy for her. Mum knew what she wanted and how she wanted it—we all came together to fulfill that wish. She is gone from her body, though not from our hearts.

In the coming days my house is filled with glorious flowers, something Mum loved, and I adore. The perfume of flowers penetrates throughout my house. Mum's funeral is the following Saturday. It is a wonderful day of celebration of her life.

She was respected and loved.

I hold the wake at my house, and it's overflowing with people, food and lots of tea and, of course, the occasional wine and beer. The atmosphere is one of a party.

Tool #6 ~
On Kindness and the Contribution to YOU

Treating others with kindness and being a contribution to the lives of others means first treating yourself with kindness and being a contribution to your own life. Why would you be unkind to yourself and put everyone else first? True kindness includes you. When you are being that energy to yourself, then there is more to give to others, and you avoid the feeling of burnout and exhaustion.

June 30th: Reflection.

Six weeks later, I don't feel anger, regret, blame, pain or guilt—only wonderful, joyous memories. There are times when there are tears, and I'm not interested in being around a lot of people or going shopping.

I notice when I tell my story it is always a great opportunity for the other person to tell their story, and maybe clear something that they hadn't seen before with the passing of their mum. There is contribution on both sides.

My writing is healing for me. It's a wonderful way to express the love I have for Mum and to see how death cannot sever love. Death, like birth, brings many changes. If you welcome those changes, much more growing can occur.

I'm enjoying the times when I have my own space to be and remember. I am being patient with myself. I know I need to tie up the loose ends of Mum's belongings so Dad doesn't need to concern himself with it. It takes time, and I'm gentle with myself in the process.

I need to gather the strength to tell people that don't know that Mum has passed away. And I need to be there for Dad and wave him goodbye on his next trip with my brothers.

I also need to ask for help instead of waiting to be asked, to remember to take care of myself and pamper myself. Being clear with what I can be for me. Being in allowance of me—not my children, husband and father—just me!

I am also aware how it is for me is only for me—no two siblings grieve the same way in response to the death of a parent. Having that awareness and allowance for family members is a great tool.

I feel lucky and thankful that I still have Dad around, though it is of little comfort to him. I see his desperation, frustration, rage, pain, loss, confusion and tears. He doesn't know what to do. I can see him asking, "Where do I go? How do I function? What is left for me?"

He comes and goes from his trips. He is in limbo. None of it takes the loneliness away. He asks, "Where do I live now?"

Dad tries to maintain his routine when he is at home. Up at 6:00 am for his early morning walk, then home for breakfast at 7:00 am to hear the rural news. Then what? His companion is gone, and it becomes a very long day. Everything is crumbling around him; all that is familiar and normal to him is gone. Change is something he has never welcomed. Mum was his rock, his foundation. He knew how to function from that place. This is the way he has done it for the last sixty years.

With all of this going on for him emotionally, he's still dealing with receiving mail for Mum like taxi subsidy forms and Aged Care Assessment Team forms. They are unaware she has passed away. How much better would it be if all departments communicated when there was a death?

We need to remove Mum's name off joint accounts, health funds and insurances. I can't do it for him with just the death certificate; he has to be present. It upsets him and is another reminder of his wife being removed from his life.

I avoid talking to others about Dad because I don't know what to do. I am there for him — but not really. I am feeling like I'm the boss of what he should do — my points of view are getting in the way. Really, what do I know about what he should or shouldn't do? I haven't lost my partner. I see now that I need to change.

I talk about this with my friends and am reminded that I am the daughter; I need to stay in the space of being Dad's daughter. Be all of me and don't ask, "What do I do?" but ask, "What can I be?" and allow him to grieve his way. Listen and maybe he'll find his way, and maybe he won't.

Tool #7 ~ No Judgment

When all is said and done and your loved one has passed, it's easy to reflect and judge yourself for all you could or should have done differently. Guilt, blame, shame, anger and rage are all conditioned distractors we use against ourselves to stop us from seeing the beauty of ourselves. In every moment we do what we can, with what we have available to us. Choice ALWAYS creates awareness, and awareness is our vehicle for growth. What you know now may not be what you knew then and going back to the past to judge yourself for the choices you made or didn't make doesn't allow you the freedom to choose today.

Judgment of yourself is unkind to you and to the people around you. Breathe deep and ask yourself, "What else is possible now?"

July 30th: Mum's Birthday.

I come back from Mum's grave. It is in the bush, about fifteen minutes away. You go through a gate, then over a gully and through another gate and come out into this peaceful setting looking over the valley.

There are only about twenty other graves there, dating back to the 1800's. I see this spot as one of Mum's gifts to me and all of us. It's an exquisite spot. As I walk back along the dirt road through the gates, I am transfixed by the gully. It is around 5:00 pm, and the sun is dropping between the trees.

The sweet perfume and freshness of the mountain air, the trees and shrubs soothe me. I smell the lilies from Mum's grave drifting down, mixing in with the freshness of the bush. As I look up the road, I see cattle and horses on the far ridges. I hear the sounds of farm life, all reminders of my incredible childhood.

I know Mum didn't care where she was buried, though this is her final gift to all of us, especially Dad. A place where nature allows our vulnerability to be, where there are no barriers, only the ability to receive it all, and be anything and everything we choose.

Life goes on and how wonderful it is to experience the many gifts of living? It truly is a choice. What do you choose? Joy and ease? Or pain and sorrow?

Epilogue

Everything is just a choice

When you are thrust unexpectedly into being a caregiver for someone you love, it's easy to feel as though you suddenly don't have choice. Suddenly, everything in life becomes about the person who is dying, and everything else has to be put on hold.

What if it *is* actually also about you?

What if the situation is about you and includes you —as well as the person you are caring for? What if there really is a choice?

Often, caring for a dying loved one is about what you should do; that you have to do it or that you are obligated to do it, rather than about making a choice to take on the role as caregiver. When you have the point of view that you have no choice, you immediately create overwhelm, conclusion and judgment, all of which stops the flow of ease. When it feels as though you don't have choice, always remember you DO have a choice. The most effective way to create awareness of what else is available to you is to ask a question:

"Is this a choice that would work for me?"

"Is this something that feels light?"

"What else is possible in this situation?"

"What role can I choose?" (Such as coordinator, communicator or social worker.)

Working together

Remember, you don't own that person, and all family members need to have time with them, even if it means delegating. Open communication is key!

A caregiver requires being aware that each family member may have a different point of view about what is best for their loved one. Everyone's target at the end is the same: "How best can we give and apply the comfort and nurturing she needs during this transition?"

I have seen many families fall apart at this time due to their own "crap" and allowing that to be enrolled into their grief.

If you receive these different points of views without judgment and be in allowance of this, you and your family members can come together as a team. This experience showed me that it can be done with ease, and we as a family became closer for it.

What is your body telling you?

Over this time with Mum at home I didn't feel well for a few days. People who I spoke with over the phone heard my voice sounding awful, so they automatically assumed I had the flu. I saw how easy it was to enroll into the story of having the flu or another illness, if I wasn't careful.

I see so much of what people say or think is actually the opposite. What if my body is trying to communicate with me and show me something?

As it was, a few days later, I felt great. I moved through the sickness without having to take anything to fix it. Yes, I had all the symptoms — severe sore throat, headache, coughing, runny nose, vomiting, aches and pains, but I rested up as much as possible, drank lots of fluids and delegated my household tasks to my kids.

What was different for me this time was there was no fear in me of, "What could happen?" This was a first, because in the past I would think, "I'd better take this, just in case," and then take all types of medicines to make me feel better.

There are addictions in life to many things. Mine was to tablets—"TO CURE IT ALL." This is an easy belief to have because it is what society continually tells us we need to do to feel better.

We don't think the body could just be telling us something or look at what is really stressing us out. Nor do we look at something that's happening in our life that we may need to change or go to the doctor to check it out further.

I have always taken tablets when I have felt unwell, especially when I got migraines. Even when I was younger after a night out, I would take a couple of Panadol before bed, "just in case" I didn't feel better in the morning.

When we talk about addiction, you often think it has to be every day, or a couple of times a week. But this isn't the case. Even if you don't have anything for three months, it is still there as your backup "just in case."

It was great to remove the backup out of my life altogether. Listening to my body is so cool.

People ask, "How do I listen to my body?"

When you get an intensity (or as most people call it, "a pain") do you hear it enough to go "ouch?" And then do you say, "What can I take to fix this?"

Instead, what about asking, "What is this? What awareness is my body telling me?" This starts to allow you to see what other possibilities there could be.

Tool #8 ~ Hands on Body Processes

Having ease with being a caregiver requires you to be consciously present in every moment and becoming fully conscious, including bringing your body along for the ride. The best way I can recommend to achieve this inclusion of your body is by receiving hands-on body processes. These nurturing, gentle treatments enhance the body's joy and functioning, facilitating an increased consciousness in the body, which allows the body to choose more ease.

This is more than relaxation and stress relief. These body processes encourage change at a molecular and cellular level, addressing the areas where you hold yourself back from being all you can be. Having body processes run regularly gives your body a sense of acknowledgment and you begin to work with your body instead of against it, allowing you to be the space required to be present.

Summary of Access Tools

Summary of Access Tools

I have shared with you some of the Access Consciousness® tools I used throughout the process of caring for Mum. Nothing can completely prepare you for the palliative care of a loved one. I hope you can find the peace and ease I found through using these tools.

Tool #1 – Ask Questions

Tool #2 – Allowance

Tool #3 – Gratitude is Greater than Love

Tool #4 – Uncreate and Destroy Your Relationships

Tool #5 – Get Your Bars™ Run

Tool #6 – Kindness and Contribution to YOU

Tool #7 – No Judgment (no guilt, no blame and no shame)

Tool #8 – Access Consciousness Body Processes™

When you are functioning from allowance and gratitude without judgment, when you are being in the question and when you have kindness for you as well as for others, then you have the space to choose whatever works for you. Be sure to stay in regular contact with friends who are rewarding and who contribute to you. And most importantly, don't compare your situation with others; every palliative care situation is different.

My Mum's Gifts

My mum's gifts will always stay with me, remind me and guide me.

Some of my favorite phrases from dear Mum:

"Don't judge others."

"There are always two sides to a story."

"No point in living in the past."

"Nobody has to know everything about you."

"Don't waste time hating or holding a grudge; move on."

"What you do with your life is up to you, not anyone else."

"Be kind and thankful."

"Don't compare."

"If it hasn't killed you, then it has made you stronger."

"No matter how you feel, get up and show up."

"Life and living is a celebration; make the best of it."

Thank you for all your gifts, Mum.

Information

Would You Like to Know More?

If you would like to get more support with caretaking a Loved one, I offer private sessions for people, to talk through different possibilities and how to make the choices that arise. If this is of interest, see:

www.kindnesswithgrief.com/services

Scan for more information

More information on Access Consciousness® tools and Bars™ can be found at:

www.accessconsciousness.com

Scan for more information

Testimonials

Wendy exudes kindness and caring and her way of being in the world empowers others to be more of who they really are. Wendy has assisted me with grief and loss issues connected with my family, and so I am very grateful for her presence and grace in the world.

~ VA, Brisbane

I remember when my dog was dying, and I would come and visit you with the dog, and it was amazing for me, because I had never had anyone put in my universe that it was even possible to have the points of view you did. That was the first time I had ever seen it.

Even though I was still sad, I just knew it was all going to be okay. And that was really different because, until then, there had been quite a lot of trauma and drama, and I would see resistance and refusal in my family about death. It was almost like it didn't exist.

I'm so grateful that you showed me there was a different reality. Because you had so much ease with me and with my dog, it gave us both something totally different. What you were doing with me was not complicated. You were just being you and showing me a different energy. That was all. And when I say that was all, it was major for me and probably tiny for you, because it was just normal for you.

~ LM, Noosa

About the Author

Wendy Mulder is an International Speaker, Grief Therapist, Access Consciousness® Certified Facilitator, Registered Nurse and author of *Learning From Grief*. With over thirty years of exposure to grief, Wendy inspires and facilitates people to a different possibility with living and dying.

She offers a range of services including private consultations and classes to assist people in moving forward with ease through grief.

"What if you see grief from a space of allowance, question and possibility?

"What if you could be in allowance of all of life?"

Wendy invites you to something different. She invites you to something that you may never have considered possible. It's a space where you can have choice, allowance and gratitude for death, for dying, for living and for you. Are you ready for a new possibility?

www.kindnesswithgrief.com

Other Books

Being You, Changing the World
By Dr. Dain Heer

Have you always known that something COMPLETELY DIFFERENT is possible? What if you had a handbook for infinite possibilities and dynamic change to guide you? With tools and processes that actually worked and invited you to a completely different way of being? For you? And the world?

The Ten Keys to Total Freedom
By Gary M. Douglas & Dr. Dain Heer

The Ten Keys to Total Freedom are a way of living that will help you expand your capacity for consciousness so that you can have greater awareness about yourself, your life, this reality and beyond. With greater awareness you can begin creating the life you've always known was possible but haven't yet achieved. If you will actually do and be these things, you will get free in every aspect of your life.

Magic. You Are It. Be It.
By Gary M. Douglas & Dr. Dain Heer

Magic is about the fun of having the things you desire. The real magic is the ability to have the joy that life can be. In this book you are presented tools & points of view that you can use to create consciousness and magic—and change your life in ways you may not even be able to imagine.

Would You Teach a Fish to Climb a Tree?
By Anne Maxwell,
Gary M. Douglas, and Dr. Dain Heer

A Different Take on Kids with ADD, ADHD, OCD and Autism. People tend to function from the point of view that there is something wrong with these children because they don't learn the way the rest of us do. The reality is that they pick things up in a totally different manner. This book takes a look at that and so much more!